BASKETBALL LEGENDS

Kareem Abdul-Jabbar

Charles Barkley

Larry Bird

Wilt Chamberlain

Julius Erving

Patrick Ewing

Anfernee Hardaway

Grant Hill

Magic Johnson

Michael Jordan

Shaquille O'Neal

Scottie Pippen

CHELSEA HOUSE PUBLISHERS

BASKETBALL LEGENDS

PATRICK EWING

Paul Wiener

Introduction by
Chuck Daly

CHELSEA HOUSE PUBLISHERS
New York • Philadelphia

Produced by Daniel Bial and Associates
New York, New York

Picture research by Alan Gottlieb
Cover illustration by Bill Vann

3 5 7 9 8 6 4 2

Library of Congress Cataloging-in-Publication Data

Wiener, Paul.
       Patrick Ewing / Paul Wiener.
             p.   cm.—(Basketball legends)
       Includes bibliographical references and index.
       ISBN 0-7910-2434-2
       1. Ewing, Patrick Aloysius, 1962-   —Juvenile literature.
       2. Basketball players—United States—Biography—Juvenile
       literature. [1. Ewing, Patrick Aloysius, 1962-   . 2. Basketball
       players. 3. Blacks—Jamaica—Biography] I. Title. II. Series.
       GV884.E9W54 1996
       796.323'092—dc20
                                                                [B]95-18496
                                                                    CIP
                                                                    AC

CONTENTS

BECOMING A
BASKETBALL LEGEND

Chuck Daly

What does it take to be a basketball superstar? Two of the three things it takes are easy to spot. Any great athlete must have excellent skills and tremendous dedication. The third quality needed is much harder to define, or even put in words. Others call it leadership or desire to win, but I'm not sure that explains it fully. This third quality relates to the athlete's thinking process, a certain mentality and work ethic. One can coach athletic skills, and while few superstars need outside influence to help keep them dedicated, it is possible for a coach to offer some well-time words in order to keep that athlete fully motivated. But a coach can do no more than appeal to a player's will to win; how much that player is then capable of ensuring victory is up to his own internal workings.

In recent times, we have been fortunate to have seen some of the best to play the game. Larry Bird, Magic Johnson, and Michael Jordan had all three components of superstardom in full measure. The brought their teams to numerous championships, and made the players around them better. (They also made their coaches look smart.)

I myself coached a player who belongs in that class, Isiah Thomas, who helped lead the Detroit Pistons to consecutive NBA crowns. Isiah is not tall—he's just over six feet—but he could do whatever he wanted with the ball. And what he wanted to do most was lead and win.

All the players I mentioned above and those whom this series will chronicle are tremendously gifted athletes, but for the most part, you can't play professional basketball at all unless you have excellent skills. And few players get to stay on their team unless they are willing to dedicate themselves to improving their talents even more, learning about their opponents, and finding a way to join with their teammates and win.

It's that third element that separates the good player from the superstar, the memorable players from the legends of the game. Superstars known when to take over the game. If the situation calls for a defensive stop, the superstars stand up and do it. If the situation calls for a big shot, they want the ball. They don't want the ball simply because of their own glory or ego. Instead they know—and their teammates know—that they are the ones who can deliver, regardless of the pressure.

The words "legend" and "superstar" are often tossed around without real meaning. Taking a hard look at some of those who truly can be classified as "legends" can provide insight into the things that brought them to that level. All of them developed their legacy over numerous season of play, even if certain games will always stand out in the memories of those who saw them. Those games typically featured amazing feats of all-around play. No matter how great the fans thought the superstars, the players were capable yet of surprising them, their opponents, and occasionally even themselves. The desire to win took over, and with their dedication and athletic skills already in place, they were capable of the most astonishing achievements.

CHUCK DALY, most recently the head coach of the New Jersey Nets, guided the Detroit Pistons to two straight NBA championships, in 1989 and 1990. He earned a gold medal as coach of the 1992 U.S. Olympic basketball team—the so-called "Dream Team"—and was inducted into the Pro Basketball Hall of Fame in 1994.

1

A CHRISTMAS MIRACLE

Boos showered Madison Square Garden. It was Christmas Day, 1985, and the New York Knicks trailed the Boston Celtics by 25 points with 6:39 remaining in the third quarter. The nationally televised game had turned into a disaster, at least from the Knicks' point of view.

Knick fans had seen this before and had a right to feel disappointed. There had been high hopes for the team before the 1985–86 season began. After all, after finishing the previous season with a dreadful 24-58 record, the Knicks had won the NBA's first lottery and drafted college basketball's best player, the 7-foot, 240-pound Patrick Ewing, during the offseason.

Ewing, known for his relentless energy, competitiveness, and intimidating shot-blocking defensive presence, was widely considered a franchise player, with the potential to have as much of an impact as the NBA's greatest centers, such as Bill Russell, Wilt Chamberlain,

Patrick Ewing made an immediate impact on the New York Knicks the first time he donned the uniform.

and Kareem Abdul-Jabbar. Moreover, he had led his college team, Georgetown University, to three NCAA college basketball championship finals. Thus, many New York fans unrealistically dreamed that Ewing, who had signed a $31 million contract, would lead the Knicks to an NBA championship in his first professional season.

But basketball is a team game and one player, however great, cannot win an NBA championship by himself. Although Ewing had played well during his first 28 professional games, the Knicks had stumbled and it quickly became apparent that the team's rebuilding process would take a few seasons. Entering the Christmas Day game with the Celtics, the Knicks had lost 19 of the 28 games they had played this far.

The Celtics were as good as the Knicks were bad. Boston enjoyed a 21-7 record and would win the NBA championship that season. Boston's starting lineup—Larry Bird, Kevin McHale, Robert Parish, Danny Ainge, and Dennis Johnson—was filled with future Hall of Famers.

Furthermore, the Celtics had won each of their last nine games against the Knicks. In short, all the experts expected the Celtics to blow out the Knicks, and midway through the third quarter they appeared to be doing just that.

The Knicks, however, refused to quit. With a ferocious, pressing defense they came storming back. For nearly four minutes New York held Boston scoreless. By the end of the third quarter the Knicks trailed by only ten points. The game was not yet over.

Patrick Ewing, who had been sitting on the bench with four fouls, returned to the game with 9:29 left in the fourth quarter. The Knicks were still losing by twelve points and seemed unlikely to catch the Celtics, a great team that rarely squandered a big fourth-quarter lead.

But Ewing had a different notion. When he entered the game he told his teammates that he wanted the ball on every play.

Over the next few minutes Ewing took control of the game. He capped a Knick fast break with a layup. He hit a jump hook from thirteen feet. He made a variety of jump shots from different parts of the court. He missed a shot but then got his own rebound and put it through the hoop. He found open teammates with sensational passes. All together, Ewing scored 18 points in the fourth quarter. When the buzzer sounded, the teams were tied. The game was going into overtime.

Only seconds into overtime Ewing limped off the court in agony with a sprained knee. On the sideline the Knicks' team doctor and trainer worked feverishly to treat the team's superstar. Sure enough, Ewing returned to the game. In Ewing's absence, however, the Knicks had fallen behind again. With only 1:09 remaining, the team called a timeout, trailing by the score of 97–92.

Following the timeout, Ewing rolled past three Celtics and scored on a magnificent finger-roll shot. He then grabbed a big rebound of a missed Larry Bird jump shot. The Knicks almost threw away the inbounds pass but Ewing managed to save it, dribble past Dennis Johnson, and deliver the ball to Trent Tucker for a three point shot. Tucker, the team's long-range specialist, hit the jumper, sending the game into a second overtime.

Larry Bird (left) and Robert Parish could not contain Ewing as the Knick center brought his team to a stirring Christmas Day victory in 1985.

Ewing put the Knicks ahead early in the second overtime, sparking a 16–1 run and the Knicks rolled to an easy victory after that. The final score was 113–104. Ewing finished with 32 points, 11 rebounds, 3 assists, 2 steals, and a blocked shot. The team victory, led by Ewing's memorable performance, was a magnificent Christmas present for Knick fans.

After the game, Ewing received much praise. K.C. Jones, the Celtics' coach, remarked that this game proved that Ewing "can score at will."

Hubie Brown, the Knicks' coach, stated that "what people saw is Patrick Ewing taking his game to another plateau. They've seen him have excellent moments, and they've seen him have big nights. But they've never seen him take over a game against a quality team."

Perhaps Rory Sparrow put it best: "You looked at Patrick Ewing emerge as a true super-star tonight."

2

FROM KINGSTON TO CAMBRIDGE

Patrick Aloysius Ewing was born in Kingston, the capital of Jamaica, on August 5, 1962. He was the fifth of seven children and grew up in a very poor neighborhood just outside of Kingston. As a child, he played soccer and cricket—the two most popular sports in Jamaica—but never basketball. Soccer was Patrick's favorite sport and he always played goalkeeper. Even at an early age he enjoyed playing defense.

Patrick's mother, Dorothy, moved to the United States in 1971. She hoped to earn some money to help her family and promised to send for her husband and children soon. With the aid of American relatives, she moved into a five-room house in Cambridge, Massachusetts, and found a job working in the cafeteria at Massachusetts General Hospital. Two years later, Ewing's father, Carl, Sr., joined her. He too found employment, making hoses for a rubber

Even in high school, greatness was predicted for Patrick Ewing.

company. Over the next several years the Ewing children joined their parents, singly or in twos. Patrick arrived in January 1975, at the age of twelve.

Before coming to the United States, Patrick had never touched a basketball and he did not even know how to play. One day, soon after moving from Jamaica, he passed a playground in Hoyt Park where some boys were playing basketball. Patrick watched the game and was asked if he would like to play. Although he did not know how to play, the boys were desperate to have one more player so they let Patrick join the game. Patrick was awkward on the court and did not play well that day but he immediately fell in love with the game. He began to play regularly and had soon improved dramatically.

Patrick played his first organized basketball in the seventh grade at the Achievement School, a remedial school in Cambridge. He was only 6'1" and played point guard but already he could dunk the basketball. By the eighth grade, he had sprouted up to 6'6" in height and his basketball play had begun to attract notice.

Patrick struggled academically in junior high school and then at Rindge and Latin High School. This was due partly to his thick Jamaican accent, as well as cultural differences between the United States and Jamaica. He kept working hard at his studies, however, in order to please his mother, who never stopped stressing the importance of education. With the help of tutoring during the school year and extra classes in the summer, Patrick greatly improved his reading and writing skills.

Meanwhile, on the basketball court at Rindge and Latin, Patrick became a star.

Patrick, however, was a shy person who did not particularly enjoy the spotlight.

By his junior year Patrick was 6'11" and weighed 205 pounds. By his senior year he had grown to seven feet tall and his weight had risen to 230 pounds. This added weight helped his basketball game. On offense he was better able to gain position near the basket and on defense he could now lean on other players and keep them away from the basket.

Through hard work and talent, Patrick—remarkably enough since he had only played the game for five years—soon became the best high school basketball player in the country. Beginning in Ewing's sophomore year, Rindge and Latin captured three Massachusetts state basketball championships. In fact, the team was so good that it only lost one game during those three years.

During the summer before his senior year, Patrick was invited to try out for the United States Olympic basketball team. Although he did not make the team, the very fact that he had even been invited to compete was an amazing achievement since no other high school basket-ball player had ever been asked to try out before.

Ewing credits much of his basketball suc-cess to his high school coach, Mike Jarvis. Jarvis preached a team-oriented game and mod-eled Rindge and Latin's style on the Boston Celtics. Jarvis felt that Ewing's potential was enormous. Indeed, he believed that Ewing could become as great as Bill Russell, the Celtics' leg-endary center, and he regularly told this to Patrick. One day Patrick, who had never before heard of Russell, finally asked Jarvis, "Who is this Bill Russell?" He wanted to make sure that the comparison was complimentary.

If Ewing credits Jarvis for much of his success, Jarvis is quick to credit Ewing. As Jarvis said: "He was a hard worker, and if he didn't know something, he'd ask you a thousand times until he got it right. He became a star and a great player, but he wasn't always a great player." During practice Ewing worked so hard that Jarvis often had to sit him down. He feared that Patrick would otherwise hurt himself or his teammates.

By his senior year, hundreds of colleges sought to recruit Ewing—who was considered a "can't miss" prospect—to play basketball. In order to organize the recruiting process, Jarvis, after consulting with Ewing and his parents, sent a letter to 150 colleges. This letter, which became known as the "Ewing Letter," indicated that Ewing would need special academic considerations, such as tutoring, special instruction and untimed tests.

Unfortunately, the letter left many basketball fans with the wrong impression that Ewing was a slow learner. As a result, during the 1981 Massachusetts high school basketball championship game against Boston College High School, he was taunted by chants of "Ewing can't read." Although these and other similar cruel chants and remarks hurt him, Ewing refused to respond verbally or let it affect his play. Instead, he relied heavily on the support of his family and friends, who knew that he was very intelligent.

Of the 80 schools that responded to Jarvis's letter, 16 were invited to make a presentation about their academic and athletic program to Ewing, his parents, Jarvis and Steve Jenkins, who coached Ewing before Jarvis. From this group of schools, Ewing pared his list to six colleges: the University of North Carolina, UCLA, Boston College, Boston University, Georgetown and Villanova.

Ewing chose Georgetown, mostly because he wanted to play for its great coach, John Thompson. Ewing felt that he could learn a lot about basketball by play-

Every college wanted Ewing to play for their basketball program. Ewing showed off the banner of the school he eventually chose.

ing for Thompson, who had himself played center for three seasons in the NBA as a backup to Bill Russell. In addition, Thompson had a reputation for making sure that his players performed well in the classroom and not just on the basketball court.

For his part, Thompson visited Ewing's home only once during the recruiting process and did not try to put too much pressure on Ewing to attend Georgetown. He also made it clear that Ewing would not receive special educational considerations if he attended Georgetown. This honest approach was appreciated by Dorothy Ewing, who took a liking to Thompson.

Despite his low-key recruiting, Thompson very much wanted Ewing to play for his team. In fact, Thompson had become enchanted with Ewing the first time that he ever saw him play— in the Massachusetts state championship game between Rindge and Latin and Boston Latin. At

*Georgetown's Coach John
Thompson had been a fine
professional center himself.*

one point during that game Thompson, who was
watching with Red Auerbach, his former coach
with the Boston Celtics, saw Ewing draw a
charge, and then moments later steal the ball
and drive the length of the court for a slam
dunk. After seeing this, he turned to Auerbach
and said of Ewing, "Get him and I'll win a championship." As it turned out, Thompson would
get Ewing to attend Georgetown and his predic-
tion came true. Ewing would indeed lead
Georgetown to a championship. For his part,
Ewing would never regret his decision to choose
Georgetown or play for Thompson, who would

become like a father to him.

Attending Georgetown, which is located in Washington D.C., meant, of course, that Ewing would be leaving Cambridge. But he would not quickly forget Cambridge, the city in which he had learned to play basketball, and Cambridge would not forget him easily. In October 1984, Cambridge awarded Patrick Ewing a key to the city. It was a very special honor for a very special person.

Several months after receiving this award, Ewing experienced a second homecoming when he visited Jamaica for the first time since his childhood. It was an emotional trip for Ewing and he was greeted by huge, enthusiastic crowds everywhere he went. To everyone's delight, Ewing ate Jamaican food and spoke in a Jamaican accent. Even though he was a rising star, Patrick Ewing had not forgotten his roots.

3

HOYA PARANOIA

Ewing adjusted quickly to college life. He lived in a dormitory with students who were not athletes and he made a lot of friends. He also worked hard on his academic subjects and managed to maintain a "B" average during his freshman year. In addition, Ewing, who majored in fine arts, spent a lot of time drawing and painting in the art studio.

But as hard as he tried, it was not possible for Ewing to lead a completely normal college life. After all, he was a seven-foot-tall basketball star who was the focus of sportswriters from all over the country.

Fortunately, Thompson protected his basketball players from the media. Most of the time, Thompson forbade Ewing and his teammates from even giving interviews, preferring that his players concentrate instead on their academic studies. Ewing appreciated Thompson's protec-

Patrick Ewing leaped so high that his head was in the net. But in this 1982 game against North Carolina, his first ever as a Hoya, he was called for goaltending five times in the first half alone.

As a congressional aide for Senator Robert Dole (left), Patrick Ewing got to meet President Ronald Reagan in the Oval Office.

tive policy since it enabled him to "go about doing things, going to school and hanging out with my friends and enjoying college life." A big problem with not talking to the press, however, was that Ewing's silence was often misunderstood. Some people wrongly believed that he was unfriendly and even hostile.

Ewing's impact on Georgetown's basketball program was immense. The Georgetown Hoyas had fielded many competitive basketball teams. The Hoyas, however, had never reached the finals or even the semifinals (known as The Final Four) of the NCAA basketball tournament—the most important tournament in college basketball. During Ewing's four years at Georgetown the Hoyas reached the NCAA finals three times.

The team's success was based primarily on an energetic and physical defense that was designed to wear down other teams and create turnovers leading to fastbreak baskets. This style of play became known as "Hoya Paranoia." At the heart of Georgetown's defense was the team's center, Patrick Ewing, who clogged the lane and forced opponents to take poor shots. In addition to his intimidating play, Ewing became known for his constant scowl on the basketball court (which intimidated opponents) and for wearing a T-shirt under his basketball jersey.

Ewing's play improved dramatically in the course of his freshman year. By the end of the year he had learned to better control his temper on the court, fight less with opposing players, use his elbows less to keep away opponents from the basket, bobble the ball less often when he received a pass, and hit his outside shots more consistently. He had also become less shy around his teammates.

In addition to Ewing, there were several other excellent basketball players on the Hoyas during Ewing's freshman season. Foremost among them was Eric (Sleepy) Floyd, an explosive offensive player, known for his graceful drives to the basket and his deadly outside shooting.

Led by Ewing and Floyd, Georgetown advanced to the NCAA finals for the first time in the school's history. Georgetown's opponent in the finals was North Carolina. It was a classic matchup as the Tar Heels featured three future NBA stars on their squad: Michael Jordan, James Worthy, and Sam Perkins. Moreover, the game matched John Thompson against Dean Smith, good friends and two of the best coaches in all of college basketball.

The final was played before 61,612 at the New Orleans Superdome, the largest crowd ever to watch a basketball game in the Western Hemisphere. And it turned out to be one of the greatest NCAA championship games ever played.

The game started dramatically as an overaggressive Ewing was whistled for four goaltending calls in the opening minutes. After that the game remained close. Just before halftime, Ewing scored on a dunk to put Georgetown ahead 32–31 at the break. Throughout the game, Georgetown's quickness on defense prevented North Carolina's players from scoring easily. The one exception was Worthy, who displayed a dazzling repertoire of explosive drives to the hoop and finished with a game-high 28 points.

With Georgetown trailing 61–58 late in the game, Ewing and Floyd hit back-to-back jump shots to give the Hoyas a one point lead. With only 18 seconds left, however, Jordan nailed a 16-foot jumpshot to put the Tar Heels on top. That left the Hoyas with one chance to win but Georgetown's Fred Brown committed a crucial turnover. The game was over. Ewing, who proved that he was becoming an offensive as well as a defensive force, had played superbly, scoring 23 points and 11 rebounds, but his team had nevertheless suffered a heartbreaking defeat.

During the summer Ewing worked on Capitol Hill as a Congressional aide to Senator Bob Dole. It was a wonderful educational experience and a good break from the pressures of playing basketball. That summer he became friendly with another aide, Rita Williams, who was working for Senator Bill Bradley. He and Williams would eventually marry.

Since Floyd had graduated, Ewing was forced to assume a greater role in Georgetown's offense during his sophomore season. Ewing responded well to the challenge and his scoring average jumped to 17.7 points per game, a five point increase from the season before. His rebound total also increased significantly, from 7.5 to 10.2 per game.

But despite Ewing's outstanding play, it was a difficult season in many respects. Ewing was taunted mercilessly, often racially. At one game fans chanted "Ewing is an ape" and at another the crowd shouted "Ewing Can't Read." T-shirts and buttons were even sold that said "Ewing Kant Read Dis."

In addition, the Hoyas had a disappointing season. After the previous season's near championship, expectations were high. But the team failed to reach the NCAA finals once again.

For Ewing, the biggest blow, however, was the sudden death of his mother, who had suffered a heart attack, in September 1983. She was only 55 years old. After her death, Ewing vowed that he would not leave Georgetown until he had graduated, even though he could have begun to earn millions of dollars in the NBA. He had promised his mother that he would receive a college degree and he intended to keep that promise.

Jim Master of Kentucky has no chance of keeping Ewing from dunking in this 1984 game.

During Ewing's junior season, Georgetown was the best team in college basketball. The addition of Reggie Williams, an exciting 6'7" freshman, helped. But the biggest factor in Georgetown's success was the play of Ewing. One statistic is particularly telling—for the season Ewing averaged four blocked shots a game. He was by now college basketball's most dominating player.

Increasingly, however, Ewing was becoming known as a "bully" on the basketball court, a label that masked his tremendous talent. Ewing disagreed with the criticism that he was too rough on the court but he refused to change his aggressive, physical style of play. As he put it: "Intimidation is part of life, it's part of basketball. The strong get stronger and the weak get weaker."

The Hoyas capped a spectacular regular season by sweeping through the NCAA tournament. Not surprisingly, Ewing played a huge role. He tapped in the game-winning basket against Southern Methodist University. He scored 16 points (including a thunderous late game two-handed dunk off an alley hoop pass), grabbed 15 rebounds and blocked 6 shots against the University of Nevada Las Vegas, leading UNLV's longtime coach, Jerry ("The Shark") Tarkanian, to remark that "Patrick's the best I've ever played against." And he so dominated Dayton defensively that after the game one Dayton player described him as "frightening, very mammoth, an octopus."

Then, in the semifinals against Kentucky, Georgetown produced one of the greatest defensive performances in the tournament's history. Trailing 29–22 at halftime, the Hoyas completely shut down the Wildcats, holding Kentucky to a total of only three second-half baskets, en route to a 53–40 victory. During one stretch, Kentucky missed 21 straight shots. For the game, the normally good-shooting Wildcats succeeded on only a miserable 24.5% of their field goal attempts.

The NCAA final matched Ewing against

another great center, and a man who would later become one of his rivals in the NBA—the University of Houston's Akeem ("The Dream") Olajuwon. (Years later, as a member of the Houston Rockets, Olajuwon, who was from Nigeria, would change his name to Hakeem.) Throughout the game both Ewing and Olajuwon were in foul trouble and they played each other evenly. Ewing's teammates, however, were too good for Houston and Georgetown prevailed, 84–75.

Georgetown had won a national championship for the first time ever. It was a fitting way to end a season in which the Hoyas had won more games (34) than any other college team in 36 years and had set an NCAA record, by holding its opponents to an all-time low shooting percentage of only 39.5 for the season. The victory also meant that Thompson became the first black coach of a Division I college basketball champion.

Ewing's sensational performance was not overlooked as he was voted Most Outstanding Player of the tournament. In addition, over the summer he finally played on the United States Olympic basketball team. He started in five of the six games and helped the United States to a gold-medal victory.

Meanwhile, off the basketball court another dramatic event occurred in Ewing's life—the birth of his son, Patrick Ewing, Jr. The mother was Sharon Stanford, his high school sweetheart.

The Hoyas dominated college basketball again during Ewing's senior year, losing only two games during the regular season. Once more, the key to the team's success was its

Ewing was proud to get his degree from Georgetown in 1985.

aggressive, pressing defense. For the season, Georgetown again held its opponents to under 40% field goal shooting (39.9) and outrebounded them by a huge average margin of 9.2 per game. In both areas Georgetown led the nation.

And Ewing's play was better than ever, as he regularly buried turn-around jumpshots, hit jump hook-shots and scored on the fast break. In addition, his assist total increased substantially.

Georgetown sailed through the NCAA tournament. After routing its rival, St. John's, Georgetown appeared headed for a second straight championship. Its opponent in the final was Villanova, a team that had lost 10 games during the regular season, including a one-sided loss to Georgetown. Led by its fiery, cigar-smoking coach, Rollie Massimino, Villanova was a "Cinderella team" that had upset many favored teams in the tournament prior to reaching the final. But very few experts gave it a chance against the defending champions.

But miracles sometimes happen and the 1985 NCAA final was one of those miracles. By playing a near perfect game, Villanova defeated Georgetown 66–64. It was the greatest upset in NCAA history. A key to Villanova's success was its ability to defend effectively against Ewing by double- and triple-teaming him throughout the game. But most unbelievable was Villanova's sensational shooting. For the game it shot a record-breaking 78.6% from the field! And this was against Georgetown, one of the greatest defensive teams of all time. Incredibly, in the second half, Villanova missed only one shot from the field. Ewing fared well but he was outplayed by Villanova's 6'9" center, Ed Pinckney. Although Ewing was bitterly disappointed by the defeat he remained gracious, clapping for Villanova after the final buzzer had sounded.

Ewing received many awards for his fine season. Among others, he won Player of the Year awards from the National Association of Basketball Coaches, the Associated Press, and the *Sporting News.*

On May 25, 1985, Patrick Ewing graduated from Georgetown, along with 1,460 classmates. He was the school's all-time leading rebounder (1,316) and shot blocker (493) and its second-leading scorer (2,184). During his four years, Georgetown had compiled an extraordinary record of 121–22, the best four-year record for a college basketball team in almost forty years. Ewing's presence at Georgetown had also earned a great deal of money; an estimated $12 million, through a tripling of attendance at games and televised NCAA play.

But for Patrick Ewing what was most important was that he had fulfilled his mother's dream. He had earned a college degree.

4

LOTTERY LUCK

It was known as the Ewing Lottery. The seven participating teams were the Atlanta Hawks, Indiana Pacers, Golden State Warriors, Los Angeles Clippers, New York Knicks, Sacramento Kings and Seattle SuperSonics. These teams had the dubious distinction of finishing the 1984–85 NBA season with the worst records in the league. As a consolation, each team logo was now going to be placed in an envelope and removed from a glass drum one at a time by David Stern, the NBA commissioner. The team whose logo was chosen first would receive the seventh pick in the upcoming NBA draft of college basketball players, the second one chosen would draft sixth and so forth. The team whose logo remained alone at the end of the lottery would draft first and obtain the rights to college basketball's best player.

The lottery was held on May 12, 1985, which

NBA Commissioner David Stern (left) and Knicks General Manager Dave DeBusschere stand by the number one pick in the 1985 draft.

was Mother's Day, at the Waldorf-Astoria Hotel in New York City. It was the first time that the NBA had ever held a lottery and there was a lot of excitement. In previous years, teams drafted college players in reverse order based on their record from the previous season. So, under the old system, the team with the fifth worst record drafted fifth. In addition, the worst team in the NBA's Eastern Conference flipped a coin with the worst team in the Western Conference to determine which team would choose first. The league finally decided to change to a seven-team lottery system since weak teams had an incentive to lose games in order to improve their drafting position.

The excitement of this lottery was particularly great because the first prize, Patrick Ewing, was so big. A player with so much potential was rare and each of the lottery teams took unusual means to insure that its logo would be the one chosen last. Before the lottery was held, the Clippers' management joked about enlisting 33 Hasidic rabbis to chant Ewing's name in unison since his Georgetown uniform number was 33. And Indiana's player personnel manager admitted that he had "thought about parapsychologists, mediums, tarot cards and Ouija boards." On the morning of the big day, several general managers attended church to say a special prayer. To the lottery itself, each team brought a unique lucky charm as well as a team jersey displaying Ewing's name.

The lottery began at approximately 2:10 p.m. and was televised live on CBS during halftime of a Boston Celtics-Philadelphia 76ers playoff game. The seven nervous general managers sat next to each other, near the commissioner and the envelopes that would decide their franchises' fates for the next fifteen years. The first envelope picked contained the logo of the Warriors, a team that had tied for the worst record in the league during the 1984–85 season, and Al Attles, the team's general manager, could not hide his disappointment. The Kings' logo appeared next, followed by the Hawks and the SuperSonics.

That left three envelopes. As David Stern opened the next one, Dave DuBusschere, the Knicks' general manager and one of the team's all-time great players, buried his head in his hands. The tension was too great. "The Los Angeles Clippers," Stern announced. Only two teams now remained with a chance to draft Ewing, the Knicks and the Pacers, a team that only two years before had lost a coin toss for the rights to draft Ralph Sampson, another center who was considered to have great potential. Stern reached for the next envelope and DeBusschere crossed his hands in front of his face, unable to look. "The Indiana Pacers. . . ." It was all over. Patrick Ewing was going to be a New York Knick.

DeBusschere, wearing a huge grin, gave a thumbs up signal and immediately pulled out a blue and orange Knick jersey with the number 33 and Ewing's name emblazoned on the back. The Waldorf ballroom, tightly packed with Knick fans, exploded. For the next two hours, Knick officers were flooded with over 1,000 phone calls requesting season ticket applications. New York, which had just suffered through a miserable 24-58 Knick season, was celebrating. The future looked bright.

5

GETTING BETTER

The Knicks signed Ewing to a contract worth $30 million over 10 years. He would earn $1.7 million in his first season, the most ever paid to an NBA rookie. Ewing, who had spent most of his childhood in poverty, was now a wealthy man.

But a big contract creates even greater expectations and, more than ever, New Yorkers now expected him to turn the Knicks into a winning team. There would be a lot of pressure on the 23-year-old Ewing.

Meanwhile, the demand for Knicks tickets soared. For Ewing's first NBA season (1985–86), the Knicks sold 11,000 season tickets, 6,000 more than the year before. The sale of these extra season tickets alone earned the Knicks approximately $3 million, far more than Ewing's annual salary.

Ewing's first professional basketball game

As a rookie, Ewing realized he could hold his own against all the best players, including Kareem Abdul-Jabbar of the Lakers.

was played at Madison Square Garden against the Philadelphia 76ers. When Ewing was introduced just prior to tipoff the sold out crowd of 19,591 roared wildly. A new era in Knick basketball had begun.

Ewing played well in his debut, scoring 18 points and grabbing 6 rebounds. He was easily outplayed, however, by the veteran Moses Malone, one of basketball's all-time great centers, who finished with 35 points and 13 rebounds, and the 76ers won, 99–89.

After the game Malone praised Ewing: "Ewing's a very smart player. He plays the game the way it should be played. He'll be a great player someday."

The loss was the first of eight straight to start the season. The Knicks would remain in last place all season. Ewing, who had always played for winning teams, quickly became depressed. As he said: "I'm never going to get used to losing."

Part of the problem was that the Knicks had lost two key players to injuries. Bernard King, who was the top scorer in the NBA before undergoing knee surgery, missed the entire season. And Bill Cartwright, a fine offensive player, who had just signed a new six-year contract with the Knicks before the season began, broke his left foot in a preseason game.

The physical pro game took its toll and Ewing suffered various injuries during the season. The first occurred in a preseason game against the Indiana Pacers when Ewing was flung to the floor by another rookie center, Steve Stipanovich, and suffered a bruised elbow. Then, in the first game of the regular season, he twisted his left ankle. Both of these injuries would continue to bother him throughout the season. In addition to these injuries, Ewing developed sore knees from the regular pounding that he endured during games.

Finally, just before the All-Star break in a game against the Utah Jazz, Ewing hurt his right knee. He missed several games and when he tried to return he reinjured the knee. On March 15, he had to have surgery. Patrick Ewing's season was over. He had only played in 50 of the team's 82 games and the team finished with a dismal 23-59 record.

Despite the losses, the difficulties of adjusting to the rigors of the NBA, and the injuries, Ewing's first season contained many highlights. There was the Christmas Day miracle comeback against the Celtics. There was also his performance against the Los Angeles Lakers, when he outdueled Kareem Abdul-Jabbar in his first head-to-head game against the legendary center. In addition, he was the only rookie to be chosen for the All-Star game (he did not play due to injury) and he won "Rookie of the Year" honors, easily finishing ahead of Xavier McDaniel of the Seattle SuperSonics and Karl Malone of the Utah Jazz. Finally, there were his impressive season averages: 20.0 points, 9.0 rebounds, and 2.1 blocked shots per game.

Ewing spent the offseason trying to rehabilitate himself. He rode a bike, lifted weights, and swam regularly. He also settled a lawsuit brought by Sharon Stanford over the amount of child support that he owed for the care of his son.

Even with Ewing's return, the Knicks once more began the season poorly. After seven games the Knicks were only 1-6 and again were in last place.

The Knicks enjoyed some good years playing under coach Rick Pitino. The players sitting behind Pitino here are (left to right): Mark Jackson, Ewing, and Kenny Walker.

Most of the criticism for the Knicks' slow start was directed at Knicks' coach, Hubie Brown. Bill Cartwright had recovered from his injury and Brown had decided to play the team's two centers, Ewing and Bill Cartwright, at the same time. This became known as the "Twin Towers" strategy.

It did not work. Ewing was forced to play forward, a position that he had never played before. He was not comfortable at forward, however, and did not play well. On defense, instead of being near the basket where he was so effective, and where he could rebound and block shots, he found himself running all over the court chasing smaller, faster forwards. And on offense, Ewing did not know where to position himself to avoid encroaching on Cartwright's space near the basket.

Ewing was unhappy with the "Twin Towers" strategy and he did not try to hide his feelings. As he said: "I'm a center. That's what I am. I'm not a forward. I miss being inside. I'm going out chasing guys like Xavier McDaniel and Terry Cummings [of the Milwaukee Bucks]. It's rough. That's not me."

After the Knicks' record reached 4-12, Brown was fired. The team's new coach, Bob Hill, immediately returned Ewing to center and Ewing's play improved considerably.

In December, Ewing played two of his finest games of the season. He scored 43 points (a career high at the time) against the Atlanta Hawks but somehow the Knicks managed to lose, 122–110.

Then, against the Chicago Bulls, Ewing pulled off the second consecutive Christmas Day miracle performance. With the Knicks trailing 85–84, Trent Tucker took what appeared to be the Knicks' final shot. Tucker missed but Ewing grabbed the rebound and, while still airborne, put in the game-winning shot as the buzzer sounded. The Knicks had won, 86–85.

Despite these magical performances and some impressive season averages (21.5 points, 8.8 rebounds per game), it was, on the whole, another frustrating season. The Knicks managed only a 20–46 record under Bob Hill and ended the 1986–87 season with a 24-58 record and another last-place finish. Furthermore, Ewing's season ended badly as he slipped on a wet spot and missed the team's final 19 games.

The 1987–88 Knicks had an exciting new look. The team had a new coach, Rick Pitino, and a talented point guard, Mark Jackson.

Ewing was thrilled with the choice of Pitino as coach. He had known Pitino for ten years, since as a ninth grader he began to watch Pitino's Boston University team practice. Later, Ewing would enroll in summer basketball camps where Pitino taught. Pitino had also been a Knick assistant coach under Hubie Brown for two seasons, although he had left the team before Ewing had arrived.

As Knick coach, one of Pitino's top priorities was to maintain a good relationship with Ewing, the team's franchise player. Unlike Brown, who often criticized Ewing in front of his teammates, Pitino was quick to praise his star player at every opportunity. As he told Ewing, "The only guy I don't get along with is someone who doesn't work hard. The only thing I ask of you is to practice." Since Ewing worked as hard as anyone, he got along very well with Pitino.

Under Pitino the Knicks played an exciting style of basketball. In particular, he regularly employed a defensive tactic known as the full-court press. The object of the fullcourt press was to force the opposing team to commit turnovers that would lead to easy baskets. This was achieved by double-teaming the opposing player who was handling the ball. For Pitino practice and preparation were the keys to mastering the fullcourt press and other successful tactics.

Pitino's aggressive style of basketball had worked well for the college teams that he had coached. He had turned bad teams at Boston University and Providence College into winners. In fact, during the previous season he had been named Coach of the Year in college basketball for guiding Providence College to a surprising berth in the Final Four of the NCAA tournament. Pitino now hoped to bring the same success to the Knicks.

Ewing also liked Pitino's upbeat personality. He felt that Pitino had brought to the Knicks some of the fun of the college game.

Another major addition was Mark Jackson, a rookie point guard from St. John's, who had frequently played against Ewing in college. Jackson was a great passer. He was particularly effective at dishing the ball to a cutting player—usually Ewing—for a slam dunk. He was also skilled at feeding the ball inside to Ewing when Ewing had good position near the basket.

The Knicks once again started the season poorly and at first it appeared that the team had improved little. As the season wore on, however, the Knicks began to master Pitino's complicated game plan. By February the team was on a roll, achieving its first winning month in four years. March proved to be another winning month.

But the Knicks saved their best play for April as they scrambled to make the playoffs. During one stretch the Knicks won five of six games, including victories over two top teams, Detroit and Atlanta. In those six games Ewing was sensational, shooting an incredible 70.4 percent field goal percentage and scoring at least 36 points in four of the games. In one game Ewing scored 41 points and grabbed 11 rebounds—in just 26 minutes of play! "I feel unstoppable," he remarked afterwards.

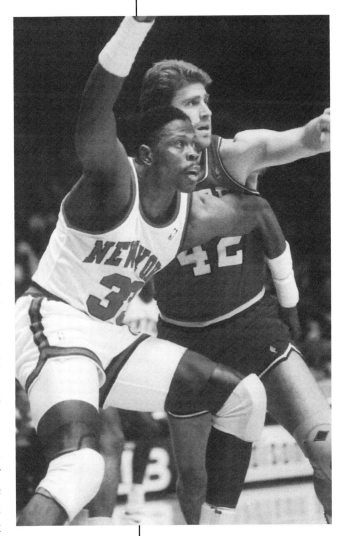

Ewing battles for position against Philadelphia's Mike Gminski in the 1989 playoffs.

The Knicks' hopes for making the playoffs came down to a single game against the Pacers in Indiana. A win, and they would make the playoffs. A loss, and the season would be over. The game was extremely close. With only four seconds remaining, the Knicks led by two points but Indiana had the ball. Steve Stipanovich drove towards the basket and took an off-balance shot. He missed and the game was over. The Knicks—despite a 38-44 record—had finally made the playoffs.

Now the Knicks had to face the Celtics in a best-of-five series. Boston easily won the first two games as Larry Bird was superb. One more Celtics' victory and the Knicks would be eliminated. But the Knicks would not quit. In front of a roaring, delirious crowd at Madison Square Garden, the Knicks won Game 3, 109–100. Ewing, who scored 31 points and had 10 rebounds, helped seal the game by hitting several big foul shots in the last two minutes. Said Ewing: "When I go to the free-throw line I just try to block everything out and concentrate on the rim. I really felt comfortable out there."

The Knicks played as hard as they could in Game 4. With only six minutes left, the Knicks led by six points. Boston called a timeout and the fans at Madison Square Garden exploded with excitement. But the game was not over. After the timeout the veteran Celtics roared back to win. Ewing finished with 20 rebounds but in the end it was not enough.

After the game, Pitino stated that he was "prouder of this team than any other team I've coached." The Knicks were once again a good basketball team.

The Knicks posted a 52–30 record during 1988–89, one of the best in the league. They also won the Atlantic Division for the first time in fifteen years.

The team was successful for several reasons. There was the offseason acquisition of Charles Oakley, a dominant offensive rebounder and scrappy inside scorer. There was the fact that

Pitino's complicated system was by now familiar to most of the team. There was the record setting three-point shooting (led by Trent Tucker) that earned the team a nickname—"The Bomb Squad." And there was the Knicks' dominant homecourt play that lasted for most of the season.

Finally, there was the overall performance of Patrick Ewing. For the most part, he continued the fine play that had elevated his team into the playoffs the season before. For the season, he averaged 22.7 points, 9.3 rebounds and 3.5 blocks per game. He shot 56.7% from the field, fourth overall in the NBA. He was twice named NBA Player of the Week. He was selected for the All-Star team and the All-Defensive team. He also received serious consideration for the league's Most Valuable Player award (placing fourth behind Magic Johnson, Michael Jordan, and Karl Malone).

The Knicks swept through the first round of the playoffs by defeating the Philadelphia 76ers in three straight close games. The Knicks' second round opponent was Michael Jordan and the Chicago Bulls. Coming off of its sweep of Philadelphia, New York entered the series with a lot of confidence. However, that confidence was quickly shaken when the Bulls captured Game 1 in overtime. Although the Knicks pulled even in Game 2, the Bulls, led by Jordan, won Games 3 and 4 to take a commanding 3–1 lead in the season series.

During the first four games Ewing had not dominated play, as he had for much of the season. The former Knick, Bill Cartwright, deserved some of the credit for this as he kept Ewing away from the basket most of the time by banging him hard. In addition, Cartwright was him-

Ewing's long arms block Larry Bird's shot in the 1990 playoffs. Ewing's play helped give an early end to the Boston Celtics' season.

self scoring and rebounding well.

With the Knicks facing elimination, the "real Ewing" suddenly emerged in Game 5. Playing with ferocious determination, he scored 32 points, grabbed 11 rebounds, and blocked 4 shots. In an incredible sequence in the game's last minute, Ewing blocked a Jordan three-point jump shot and then raced downcourt to score on a lead pass from Mark Jackson. The Knicks won, 121–114.

Then, in Game 6, with the Knicks trailing by four and only nine seconds remaining, Trent Tucker miraculously scored a four-point play—hitting a three-point shot as he was fouled—to tie the game. Jordan, however, spoiled the dramatic comeback by hitting two last-second foul shots. It was a heartbreaking loss.

"It just didn't happen for us," said Ewing, who had scored 22 points and had 13 rebounds, after the game. "I hate all defeats. I don't like any of them. Never did, never will." A fine Knick season was over.

During the offseason Pitino accepted an offer

to return to college basketball and coach the University of Kentucky. The new Knick coach was Stu Jackson, who had been Pitino's assistant.

Under Jackson, Ewing had his finest season. He finished third in the league in scoring (28.6 points) and fifth in rebounding (10.9). He averaged 4.0 blocks per game. He set two all time Knick season records by scoring 2,347 points and blocking 327 shots. He scored at least 20 points in 73 of the Knicks' 82 games and, during one stretch, he scored 20 or more points in 28 consecutive games!

He also had two memorable regular-season performances. In November he scored 44 points and added 24 rebounds in a victory over the Golden State Warriors. And, in March he torched the Celtics for a career-high 51 points. Not surprisingly, he was chosen as the all-NBA first team center for the season.

Ewing's explosive scoring was due in part to Stu Jackson's game plan. Unlike Pitino, who designed the Knick offense to revolve around scoring transition baskets and three-point shots, Jackson preferred a more traditional approach—to get the ball to his center, close to the basket. Once he got the ball, Ewing was so effective because he had developed a variety of superb inside moves as well as a deadly outside jumpshot. In addition, he was an excellent passer. It was the combination of all these skills, plus hard work and excellent defense, that had enabled Ewing to become a superstar.

Nevertheless, despite Ewing's play, the Knicks' record slipped to 45-37. The Knicks finished third in the Atlantic Division.

The Celtics, who had won the division, blew

Ewing grabs a rebound away from Bill Laimbeer in the 1990 playoffs. But Detroit ousted the Knicks and went on to win the NBA championship.

the Knicks out in the first two games of the playoff's opening round. At that point, the Knicks' chances of advancing further seemed doomed, especially after Oakley openly criticized Ewing for not working hard enough during the first two games of the series.

But Ewing, and the Knicks, bounced back. Stung by Oakley's criticism, Ewing responded with 33 points and 19 rebounds in Game 3 and with 44 points (on 18 of 24 shooting) and 13 rebounds in Game 4. The Knicks won both.

A deciding game would be played in Boston where the Knicks had lost 26 straight times. Few experts gave the Knicks much of a chance. However, led by Ewing's 31 points, the Knicks pulled off a memorable upset. "It's destiny," he said.

But the Knicks were not destined to advance any further, as they fell to the eventual NBA champion Detroit Pistons, four games to one. In the Knicks' sole victory, Ewing scored 45 points.

During the summer, Ewing married Rita Williams, who was now a law student at Georgetown. They would have two children together, girls named Randi and Corey.

Ewing had another fine season in 1990–91,

scoring 26.6 points and grabbing 11.2 rebounds per game. He finished in the top five in the league in scoring, rebounding and blocked shots. He also had the best passing season of his career, averaging 3.0 assists per game, an extremely high number for a center.

The team, however, dropped to only 39-43 and was swept by the Bulls in the first round of the playoffs. After the final game of the series, the non-sellout crowd at Madison Square Garden began to chant, "Goodbye, Patrick." Out of frustration, the fans were blaming Ewing for the team's poor performance. Ewing tried to remain philosophical. "No one wants to be booed, but I've learned to live with it. I can't do anything about it. I'm out there giving 110 percent," he said.

6

THE RILEY ERA

Two major events happened in the Knick off-season. Pat Riley became the new head coach and Patrick Ewing signed a new, long-term contract with the team.

For most of the summer it seemed that Ewing would not remain a Knick. On June 21, three weeks after Riley was hired, Ewing filed for arbitration. He claimed that he was no longer one of the NBA's four highest paid players as his contract required and, therefore, was a free agent. As a free agent he would be free to sign with any other team.

The Knicks challenged Ewing's claim that he was not one of the league's four highest paid players. On July 22, an arbitrator heard Ewing's case and seven days later decided in favor of the Knicks.

Ewing was still a Knick but he was an unhappy one. He was tired of New York's

Ewing and Charles Smith console a dejected John Starks as the Bulls beat the Knicks in the 1993 semi-finals.

demanding fans and media. He was also tired of playing for a team that was not close to winning a championship. The Knicks listened to trade proposals for their franchise player but nothing acceptable was offered.

Meanwhile, Riley met with Ewing to try to convince him to remain with the team. Riley had joined the Knicks because he believed that the team had the potential to win a championship. But he knew that the Knicks could not win without Ewing.

Just before training camp began Ewing changed his mind and decided that he wanted to remain with the team. He and the Knicks quickly agreed to a new multi-year contract. "New York is a great town," he said. "I started my career here and I definitely would like to finish it here. But I wanted the Knicks to do the right things to ensure that we'd be an elite ball club." By signing Riley and Ewing, the Knicks had taken two giant steps in that direction.

As a coach, Riley's success was legendary. In his nine years as Lakers coach, Los Angeles had won four NBA championships, reached the NBA finals seven times and won the Pacific Division nine times. He now hoped to bring that same winning tradition to the Knicks.

Riley immediately set about to transform the Knicks into the team he wanted—the hardest working, best conditioned, and most unselfish team in the game. He was a fanatical believer in preparation and his lengthy practices, which were closed to the media, were grueling. In addition, he believed in communicating regularly with each player so that each understood their unique role on the team. He was also not afraid to criticize any player if he felt it was warranted,

even a superstar such as Ewing.

In only his first season, Riley turned the Knicks into an outstanding team. New York compiled a 51-31 record and tied Boston for first place in the Atlantic Division. Its success was due primarily to tough, physical defense and excellent rebounding. On offense the Knicks relied on regularly passing the ball inside to Ewing, who either took the shot or passed the ball back outside.

The Knicks faced the Pistons in their opening playoff round. In Game 3, Ewing hit a twelve-foot jumpshot with 13 seconds left to tie

Hakeem Olajuwon of the Rockets always was one of the toughest opponents for Patrick Ewing. Olajuwon's magnificent play on offense and defense in the 1994 finals spelled disappointment for Ewing and the Knicks.

the game. The Knicks won in overtime and eventually captured the series, three games to two.

The Knicks, however, appeared to have little chance of advancing past their next opponent, the Bulls. Chicago had a sensational regular season record of 67-15 and, entering the series, had won 18 of their last 20 playoff games. But the Knicks did not quit. In the opening game the Knicks won a stunning upset victory as Ewing scored 34 points, including a running five-footer that put the Knicks ahead for good.

Then, in Game 6, with the Knicks facing elimination, he rose to the occasion again. Ewing had sprained his ankle in the third quarter. However, he boldly limped on to the court for the final twelve minutes and scored 11 crucial points to lead the Knicks to victory. It was a memorable performance.

Even though the Bulls won Game 7, the Knicks took pride in their accomplishment. They had scared the mighty Bulls and had established themselves as a quality team.

The following season the Knicks won 60 games, tying a franchise record for wins set by the 1969–70 Knick championship squad. For the first time in Ewing's NBA career, the Knicks seemed poised to win a championship.

In the Eastern Conference final of the playoffs, the Knicks won their first two games against the Bulls, their old nemesis. Only two more wins and the Knicks would reach the NBA finals. Knick fans were confident and quietly began to celebrate.

But the celebrating quickly stopped as the Bulls evened the series with two straight victories. Game 5 at Madison Square Garden was now pivotal.

The game was tight throughout. With seconds remaining, the Knicks trailed by one but had the ball. Ewing drove the lane and passed to Charles Smith, the Knicks' 6'10" forward, who was underneath the basket. Smith's shot was blocked by Horace Grant. The ball came right back to Smith but Jordan knocked it away from behind. Smith recovered the ball but once again his shot was blocked, this time by Scottie Pippen. The ball squirted back to Smith but once more Pippen blocked his shot. The Knicks had lost. Chicago then closed out the series with a home victory. A great Knick season had ended on a sour note.

The Knicks won 57 games during the 1993–94 season but struggled through the playoffs. The Knicks' opponent in the Eastern Conference finals, the Indiana Pacers, played a similar physical, defensive style of basketball.

Game 3 of the series was a notable disaster for both the Knicks and Ewing. The Knicks scored only 68 points, the fewest ever in a playoff game during the era of the 24-second shot clock. For his part, Ewing missed all ten of his field goal attempts and scored only one point. Only once before could Ewing ever remember being held to a single point in a basketball game—during his first game for Rindge and Latin High School.

As usual, however, Ewing bounced back. In the series' decisive Game 7, he scored 24 points and added 22 rebounds and he dominated down the stretch. The Knicks won, 94–90.

The Knicks' opponent in the NBA finals was the Houston Rockets, led by Hakeem Olajuwon. Ewing and Olajuwon had faced each other once before in a final—when Georgetown had defeat-

After the Knicks defeated the Indiana Pacers in the seventh game of the Eastern Conference finals in 1994, Ewing celebrated with the crowd. Up next: the Houston Rockets.

ed the University of Houston to capture the 1984 NCAA crown. Since turning pro, however, neither of these two great centers had played on an NBA championship team.

Playing against Olajuwon would be a difficult assignment for Ewing. Olajuwon had explosive offensive moves and extraordinary defensive skills. In recent years Olajuwon had usually, but not always, outplayed Ewing in head-to-head matchups.

During the series Ewing played Olajuwon more or less evenly. While Olajuwon scored more points (26.9 to 18.9 per game), Ewing had more rebounds (12.4 to 9.1 per game).

In the end, the Rockets triumphed four games to three as Houston's reserves played extremely well. The Knicks' championship quest would have to wait.

The Knicks won 55 games during the 1994–95 season but the team's play was inconsistent. The "real season," however, did not begin until May when the playoffs started. Many believed that this would be the team's last good chance to win. After all, Ewing was almost 33 years old—past the prime of most basketball players.

After defeating the Cleveland Cavaliers, the Knicks faced the Indiana Pacers in the second round of the playoffs. It was a rematch of the previous season's grueling series and it would turn out to be one of the most exciting playoff series in NBA history.

Indiana won the opening game in spectacular fashion. With only 17 seconds remaining, the Knicks—playing with the home-court advantage—led by six points and seemed to have the game in the bag. But Reggie Miller, Indiana's sensational shooting guard, pulled a minor miracle. He hit a three-point shot, then stole the ball off the inbounds pass and bombed another three-pointer to tie the game. Miller then hit two foul shots for the Pacers' victory. It was a devastating defeat for New York.

New York bounced back to win the next game, but then Indiana won its first two games at home. Another loss would send New York packing. To make things worse, Ewing was hob-

Dale Davis of the Indianapolis Pacers had no chance on the play. But Ewing's last-second finger-roll—a shot he made 99 times out of 100 — fell just short and allowed the Pacers to move on in the 1995 playoffs.

bled with a sore left calf and had to wear a tightly wrapped compression bandage during games. The painful injury clearly affected his jumping ability and aggressiveness.

Game 5 was a close affair. With only 5.9 seconds left, Indiana's Byron Scott hit a three-point shot to put the Pacers ahead by one. The Knicks were potentially down to their last shot of the season.

In the Knicks huddle, Ewing delivered a simple message to Pat Riley: "Give me the ball." Riley agreed and ran a play for Ewing. It began with Anthony Mason's inbounds pass to John Starks, who then pushed the ball ahead to Ewing near the top of the key. Ewing put the ball on the floor, spun, took two steps towards the basket and shot. "I had made up my mind, I was going to get the ball and drive," Ewing said later. "I was either going to get fouled or make the shot. His seven-footer sailed through the basket and the Knicks had survived, though barely.

Game 6 was played in Indianapolis. The Knicks won, 92–82. It was an emotional win before a hostile crowd and was further proof of the team's tremendous character and heart. Ewing led the way with a huge 25-point, 15-rebound performance. "We just believe in ourselves," he said afterwards.

The series finale was another nailbiter. Once again, the outcome hinged on a last-second play by the Knicks. With five seconds remaining and New York trailing by two, Ewing received the inbounds pass. With a terrific display of skill, Patrick burst past two Pacers players and found himself shockingly open. He soared towards the basket, too far for a slam dunk, but near enough for a trademark finger-roll. The ball went in the hoop—and bounced out. The horn sounded, and the Knicks' season was over.

A disconsolate Anthony Mason commented in the lockerroom that "99 times out of 100, Patrick makes that shot." He knew, as did the rest of the Knicks, that no matter how hard you try for something, sometimes luck plays a role that you cannot control. The Knicks could say yet again that they had played their hearts out, but it wasn't quite enough. In the offseason Pat Riley left the Knicks in a graceless fashion.

The 1995-96 season opened with Ewing playing in his 760th game as a Knick, which moved him into first place ahead of Walt Frazier on the club's all-time list. The game also marked Don Nelson's debut as the Knicks' new head coach; but Nelson never quite got the team to accept his concept of how basketball should be played, and he failed to last the entire season. Jeff Van Gundy replaced him after 59 games but was unable to guide the Knicks to the 50-win mark for a fifth straight year. They fell three victories short.

Even so, Ewing was his usual reliable self, finishing seventh in the league in rebounding and blocked shots and ninth in scoring. And he was just as steady during the playoffs, which saw New York sweep the Cleveland Cavaliers in the opening round before falling to the eventual NBA champs, the Chicago Bulls, in a tightly contested five-game series.

Following the season, the Knicks went about retooling the team that Riley had helped build. Having already traded Charles Smith a few months earlier, they also dealt Anthony Mason and Hubert Davis. New to their roster were Larry Johnson and a pair of free agent guards: Chris Childs and Allan Houston.

Ewing, however, remained at the center of the Knicks' plans—and for good reason. Having been selected an NBA All-Star for a club-record 10th time, he was still one of the premier players around. Moreover, his desire to win was as strong as anyone's in the league. Entering his 12th NBA season, Patrick Ewing still had, as Pat Riley had put it, the "heart of a warrior."

STATISTICS

PATRICK EWING

Year	G	FG%	REB	RPG	AST	STL	BLK	PTS	AVG
1985-86	50	.474	451	9.0	102	54	103	998	20.0
1986-87	63	.503	555	8.8	104	89	147	1356	21.5
1987-88	82	.555	676	8.2	125	104	245	1653	20.2
1988-89	80	.567	740	9.3	188	117	281	1815	22.7
1989-90	82	.551	893	10.9	182	78	327	2347	28.6
1990-91	81	.514	905	11.2	244	80	258	2154	26.6
1991-92	82	.522	921	11.2	156	88	245	1970	24.0
1992-93	81	.503	980	12.1	151	74	161	1959	24.2
1993-94	79	.496	885	11.2	179	90	217	1939	24.5
1994-95	79	.503	867	11.0	212	68	159	1886	23.9
1995-96	76	.466	806	10.6	160	68	184	1711	22.5
Totals	835	.516	8679	10.4	1803	910	2327	19,788	23.7

PLAYOFF STATISTICS

Year	G	FG%	REB	RPG	PTS	AVG
1987-88	4	.491	51	12.8	75	18.8
1988-89	9	.486	90	10.0	179	19.9
1989-90	10	.521	105	10.5	294	29.4
1990-91	3	.400	30	10.0	50	16.7
1991-92	12	.456	133	11.1	272	22.7
1992-93	15	.512	164	10.9	382	25.5
1993-94	25	.437	293	11.7	547	21.9
1994-95	11	.513	106	9.6	209	19.0
1995-96	8	.474	85	10.6	172	21.5
Totals	97	.476	1,057	10.8	2180	22.5

G	games
FG%	field-goal percentage
REB	rebounds
RPG	rebounds per game
AST	assists
STL	steals
BLK	blocks
PTS	points
AVG	average

PATRICK EWING
A CHRONOLOGY

1962   Born in Kingston, Jamaica, on August 5

1975   Moves to Cambridge, MA, where he starts to play basketball

1981   Leads his Rindge and Latin High School basketball team to its third consecutive state championship

1983   Leads Georgetown University to its first finals of the NCAA championship; serves as a Congressional aide to Senator Bob Dole

1984   Georgetown wins the NCAA championship; Ewing is voted Most Outstanding Player of the Tournament; Ewing wins a gold medal playing with the United States Olympic basketball team

1985   Georgetown again reaches the finals of the NCAA tournament; Ewing is named Player of the Year by the National Association of Basketball Coaches, the Associated Press, and the *Sporting News*; the New York Knicks use their number one draft pick to choose Ewing

1986   Wins Rookie of the Year honors

1989   Leads the Knicks to its first Atlantic Division title in 15 years

1990   Has his best year statistically, setting Knicks records with 2,347 points and 327 blocks; also scores a career-high 51 points in a game against the Boston Celtics; although the Knicks beat the Celtics in the playoffs, they continue to have little success in the postseason, losing to Detroit

1994   Knicks finally get to the NBA championship series, only to lose to the Houston Rockets in seven hard-fought games

SUGGESTIONS FOR FURTHER READING

Heisler, Mark. *The Lives of Riley*. New York: Macmillan, 1994.

Kavanagh, Jack. *Patrick Ewing*. Hillside, NJ: Enslow Publishers, 1992.

Newman, Matthew. *Patrick Ewing*. Mankato, MN: Crestwood House, 1986.

ABOUT THE AUTHOR

Paul Wiener is a freelance writer and a passionate sports fan. In his spare time, he is also a lawyer. The author of *JOE MONTANA* in Chelsea House's Football Legends series is a graduate of Columbia University and Harvard Law School. He and his wife Elizabeth live in New York City.

INDEX

PICTURE CREDITS
Reuters/Bettmann: pp. 2, 53, 56; UPI/Bettmann: pp. 8, 12, 22, 27, 32, 36, 40; AP/Wide World Photos: pp. 14, 19, 30, 43, 46, 48, 50, 58; Courtesy Georgetown University: p. 20; Ronald Reagan Presidential Library: p. 24.